HOW TO LIVE WITH MAMMALS

HOW TO
LIVE WITH
MAMMALS

Ash Davida Jane

Victoria University of Wellington Press

VICTORIA UNIVERSITY OF
WELLINGTON
TE HERENGA WAKA

Victoria University of Wellington Press
PO Box 600 Wellington
New Zealand
vup.wgtn.ac.nz

A catalogue record is available at the National Library of New Zealand.

ISBN 9781776564163

Acknowledgements
Thank you to the editors of the following publications, in which a number of
these poems have previously appeared: *Best New Zealand Poems, Food Court x
Sweet Mammalian, Landfall, Mayhem, NZ Poetry Shelf, Peach Mag, Salty, Scum,
The Spinoff, Sport, Starling, Sweet Mammalian, Turbine | Kapohau* and *Verb Journal.*

Published with the support of a grant from

Printed in Singapore by Markono Print Media Pte Ltd

For my sister

Contents

hot bodies

how does anyone remember anything
in this heat   the cicadas scream
like they're burning alive   the footpath
is scattered with their tiny husks
they crunch when you step on them
      though you try not to   all the plants
have gone to seed too early & there'll be no food
left for March   we're left gorging ourselves
on too-red tomatoes as we race to put our
teeth in them before they rot
      they turn our stomachs   we'll be starving
come winter   how vintage
      this is not the end   the houses
are burning   right down to the roots
of the trees they were built from   every day
there's another story   it isn't going
to get any easier but you still have to
tell the kids   there is hope   you still
have to tell your friends to recycle
their beer bottles at the end of the night
      you have to fill a piñata with apology
notes   you have to open all the windows
on the windiest day & watch the curtains dance
like giant women in white dresses
      their hands reaching out to collect
the dust motes in golden rivers
the sun glancing through the windows
as sharp as cut glass   as gritted teeth
at night make our jaws ache   when we bathe in the sun

mid-afternoon   sunglasses on
      bodies stretched out & helpless

bat secrets

i find it hard to believe that everybody else
has just as many thoughts about themselves
as i do about myself
how would anything ever get done
do you love me even when i am not
dreaming of rescuing ducklings
i am not unlike the dog on the beach
digging an important hole
while the sun stays high in the sky
held up by a garter
what would Gertrude think of me
with my poor art collection
and mostly complete sentences
what will i think about when i'm 83
scientists are desperately studying bats
to figure out how they live so long for their size
so we too can enjoy an extended lifespan
but i want only the exact amount of time i have
anything more seems a waste of limited resources
(such as clean underwear)

fancy jam

growing up feels like dancing in a silent room
where everybody else is Armie Hammer

& every now & then Armie Hammer catches your eye & waves
but when you wave back you realise he was actually looking at
    Armie Hammer behind you

growing up is dying, slowly & in excruciating pain
you can't even find a good song to play at your funeral

while they carry your body to the grave in a cardboard box
with a plastic souvenir fridge magnet over each eye

because you suspect they might be the fashionable currency
in the afterlife, & you'll be damned if you let them go to waste

sometimes when you get bored of dancing
Armie Hammer takes you back to his for the night

but he always calls you Armie in bed
and never makes you cum

growing up feels like play-acting in the 80s
when happiness was something you could at least put a deposit on

you make me want to take out a mortgage with you, boy
get up early every day and walk the dogs past the white fences

paint our front door red and say
that's our house there, the one with the red door

live in our big house with the big windows
that we didn't even have to give up our art for

look back on our time amongst mould–glazed walls
with hazy nostalgia

sleep naked even in the middle of winter
and warm our hands on each other's stomachs

buy fancy jam and slowly pay off our mortgage
as we get closer and closer to death

then get up and mow the lawn
with a lawnmower we picked out together and bought brand new

we grow tomatoes

in the first place we make a home   we buy round plastic pots &
fill them with spoonfuls of earth   we dig cradles in the centre
for the seedlings to sit in   we cover the roots with blankets
of dirt & tuck them in   we say goodnight   we water them daily
pouring cup upon cup onto the dry soil   so it sinks deep & calls
the roots home   we snip off the laterals when they appear
in the elbows & knees   we tie ribbons around the stems &
anchor them to bamboo backbones   we come home drunk & I
kiss the tiny green fruit starting to form   we come inside   & our
hands smell alive and bitter   try to find perfume in a bottle this
fucking fresh   we throw parties & tell the guests   don't
put out your cigarettes in the tomato plants   one of these
babies is worth ten of you   look at the painted green of those
new leaves   the point where the stems meet in a perfect angle

we go to work

& come home at different times   I kiss your sleeping forehead when I go to bed
& you kiss mine when you wake   we leave soft touches on voicemail
hold them tightly to the chest to echo back   . . . *missed u again I miss u*
this space we share is full of   half-drunk cups of tea shining crescent
moon reflections of the ceiling lights   the basil plants we are growing in earnest
sway adoringly with the wind &   release a heady cloud of sweet perfume
the clothes dryer an absurd art piece living   in the living room
our underwear on permanent exhibition   but we are rarely two bodies
in each other's presence   doing more than always leaving
we're wedded to our jobs   sometimes people stay married because they
can't afford to pay rent on their own   your job doesn't pay enough
attention to you   it forgets to tell you it loves you
& it never puts the toilet seat back down   capitalism is a fuckboy
it can't love you like I can   it doesn't know how to treat a girl right
it's all false confidence   & ugly expensive hats

blue ladybirds

didn't it used to be so cool
to be alive   everything
was shiny   like in
a gold-leaf renaissance painting
but without all the ugly
babies
                    every day was
somebody's birthday   if
you are reading this it was
your birthday   now
nobody tells me when
their birthday is
                          i used
to see so many worms all
the time   pink wriggly
earthworms taking a risk
crossing the footpath on a
hot day
                    in primary school
we fancied ourselves proud
owners of pet ladybirds
we'd pluck them off the trees
with care   diamantes
that crawled around our
wrists and up our arms
              i could never understand
why they didn't just fly away
        i thought all ladybirds
were blue

                         i thought
people lived in rooms
carved out under the traffic lights
changing the colours
             that could be me one day
sitting up all night peering
through a periscope to make sure
nobody crashes
                         i'd
have so much time to think
about things to look forward to
             like living in my own house
             which i'd be able to buy
with my own money
                         like wearing
lipstick and going out dancing
like they do in the movies
             and instinctively knowing
the moves to the
rigorously choreographed
routine
                   coming home
at sunrise   and stepping
into the garden
             where the ladybirds
are just waking up
             more of them
than ever   thousands
and thousands   glinting
like tiny mirrors
             pushing away the dark

walking with Dorothy

a dog bothers the scraps
of food around the compost bin
        it howls at the murmur of the village stream
ignoring the voice calling from the hill
the trees gleam with overnight rain
        each tree, taken singly, was beautiful
the bees emerging
from their wooden house
mistake me for
a flower and for
a moment I am one
hopelessly lacking in pollen
swaying in the breeze
and taking up space
standing still in the mud
unmaking myself amid
leaves I've seen a thousand times
and never wondered the names of
        some trees putting out red shoots
        query: what trees are they?
a fantail flits from branch to branch
something bigger than language
in its movements
which lose
their sheen when captured
and later the sky between
apartments and streetlamps
empties but for the full moon
and Venus striving to be seen

as brightly

all the heavens seemed in one perpetual motion
grit on the footpath like glitter
the roads very dirty
a morepork somewhere in the dark
oblivious to me and better for it

observations

on a cold day i learn how only single-celled organisms
directly receive the world, their sense impressions unedited, unlike ours

so as grey as the sky looks, a murky pool, there are things i don't see,
    glimmers
of textured silver, a degree of beauty beyond the human scope

i don't know how i am supposed to go about my day like normal
knowing that i am missing out on the sounds bees make
when they bump into each other, no less real than me saying sorry
when somebody walks into me

i think about what else we are blind to, certain notes in the breadth of
    birdsong,
ultraviolets or infrared light, warming through the skin of cold-blooded
    animals

and what other things might slip away, if we try to take in all the vast
layers at once, spread our minds so far they grow thin as lace,
gaps widening where once there were the faintest scents, the whisper of
    fresh rain

and before i go out into the world i check the weather forecast again,
i try to imagine the sky flooded ultraviolet, and then without any light at all

i put on my three layers, and one griefproof layer, and i step outside

conversation / conservation

standing in a room with 50 other people   we make intense
eye contact one by one   then look away
                    we talk about trivial things   & gradually
get louder & louder to be heard over the bus noise outside
          until we're shouting   so what do you do
at the tops of our lungs

                              we imagine our bodies
as aquariums for aquatic frogs   & sometimes
they surface for air in the throat-shaped part   though
they also enjoy swimming around in the stomach-shaped part
          we'd keep pet fish in tanks
in live-in submarines   complete with realistic
sea grass & a small log   what if bird-watching
was a two-way activity   what would they think of me
on the porch with tired eyes & a comically large handheld fan
          do they think the ladder in the middle of the garden
is for them to get down from the sky

                                        this room is too
big for this many conversations   the words float off
before we can get a hold of them   somebody tells me
their name but it escapes so I just nod & smile   &
watch as it joins the others   flocking in the corner
talking amongst themselves   letting us rehearse our
animal instincts &   waiting for us to do something

phosphorescent animals

    the border between body
and unbody is a fluid line   wavering with
the currents   and the waves flow in and out
like air in colossal lungs   salt embeds itself in your
fingernail beds   the fingers themselves
contract and expand   hot blood under the skin
            glowing blue

   a firefly   or the moon
      rises above the surface
its edges a blur of gold light through the
shifting water and the thick film that
  pulls with it
       a ghost   drifting
in the sea

the girdle of Venus
is a long translucent animal   a ribbon
of jelly
     in distress

it lights up like a glowstick
      propelling itself forward with
row upon row of combs
   fingers like tiny hairs
     so far from human we
cannot fathom them   you
drag your arms through the water
and get caught in strands of plastic   like gossamer

they wrap themselves around you
they twist and turn in gauzy white
and catch the light
      draw the eye to your hands   the skin
      delicate and thin
         soon the ocean surface thickens
it blocks the moonlight
         everything goes dark
except for the girdle of Venus
      winding around your waist like a bioluminescent belt
terrified into light and
      flickering
         lines of blue

location, location

if Venus used to be our dream place   what's
the use in looking elsewhere   she had it all
          surface water   habitable temperatures
close to the best schools   (all on Earth)
plenty of sunlight

                              we could have begun
afresh there   built an entire public transport
system   and houses in a mix of postmodern
and high-tech architecture   found new ways to
ruin our lives   and celebrated a handful of new
holidays   such as landing day   first-
birth-on-Venus day   even Venus day
where everybody leaves the lights off
for 5832 hours
                    we could've watched Earth turn
brown   and over time stopped visiting so much
the commute is costly and we want to remember it
in its prime   not losing teeth and growing gaunt
          it's like making something solid see-through
we don't want to see its nervous system   we don't
want to see each other's hearts   plain red meat laid bare

Lindsay Lohan and I

the sign that says *only you can prevent forest fires*
instills me with a terrifying sense of responsibility
      I'm forced to really look at myself and ask
if I can handle it   is this how it feels to come face-to-face
with yourself   like Lindsay Lohan in *The Parent Trap* (1998)
     a sudden confrontation with her own existence
something most people only experience diluted   in their reflection
or a silhouette always turning away   not on summer camp
while being inexplicably good at fencing   you can take
the girl out of the 90s   in fact you don't have a choice
     time is passing and   the list of things you don't know
keeps getting longer   why would the divorced parents send their kids
to a camp so far away   instead of one closer to home
    how fast does a forest burn   how many 11-year-olds
watched this film and then   pierced their friends' ears
with a sterilised needle and an apple slice   there are hundreds
of nameless birds flocking around us   I can't google
fast enough to find out what to call them   all I can do
is stand and point   looking at myself looking at them

all the other animals are in their prime

every single one of them and i
i am hauling myself along

hoping they will not notice my aching body
in its vulnerable state

hoping they are too busy
admiring each other's plumage

or building beautiful homes
watching the nature documentary

we learn how each species of firefly
lights up in its own unique pattern

their tiny insect bodies so big
in perfect resolution

i want to look at you and ask
if you would light up for me

would you light up for me . . . every day
would you perform strange but endearing mating rituals

that David Attenborough could explain
in a kind and patient tone

some mammals adapt quickly
to changes in our human world

wild dogs in Moscow take the metro
into town to search for food

they sit politely under the seats
until the train arrives at their stop

when i first read about it i wonder
if the guards try to stop them getting on for free

but that's ridiculous
they don't have any money

i worry about Christmas lights
that flash on and off in complex patterns

i worry that the fireflies will be drawn
to their seductive glow

then i worry i am being condescending
to the fireflies

i worry about the dogs when the metro stops running
and leaves them standing on the platform for hours

waiting for the train to arrive
so patient and so hungry

in my memory it is always daytime

in my memory it is always daytime, midsummer, and you and i are lying on the bed in that trapped room, the sun drawing stripes on our skin through the blinds. they were moments of sweetness in the worst summer of our lives. we don't get to choose what we remember. i'm scared of the things i will forget. one of my earliest memories is the time i answered the phone and spent 20 minutes telling a stranger she was my mum when it was just some other woman with the same name. do you picture the world. how it changes an ear to have it filled with birds' chirping all day. i'm scared of turning bitter. i always want the possibility of running through a field and into somebody's arms. we can see in our memories a species laid bare, the nakedness of our wants. i think i'm in control but this has already been decided. to see the future all you have to do is look around. every raindrop is prophetic, a crystal ball. they cascade down and shatter on the concrete. if you listen closely you can hear the breaking. walls amplify it, brick and glass. it sounds softer in the bush, where it soaks into the undergrowth. a memory of the groundwater, splintered.

bird currency

I burst into tears and you   get out the video camera
    let's practise paying rent until we can do it
just right   let's move our bodies awkwardly so it looks
like we don't know what we're doing on purpose
    let's throw the lemmings off a cliff and tell
everyone they jumped   it'll look good in the final
cut   juxtapose it with scenes of me ugly
crying   put the sorrow right next to itself and watch
what it does   it gets bigger   it breathes
slowly in and out   it notices you watching and
tells you to fuck off
    don't you have anything better to do
practise building houses until you have somewhere
to live   practise writing things down until you think
you know which two words go next door   but wait
    it's a revolution   any two words can sit together
like   bird currency   crying establishment
disco teeth   take something you love
and empty it   press it flat
like a flower   make it dead trying to make it
yours   pin wings to a corkboard while the insect
is still alive   the butterflies
don't care for any god   cut open a body to find out
what's inside   what if we don't find anything
maybe that one was a dud   cut open another
and another   it's like a magic
trick   if you practise enough times you'll learn how
to make the rabbit come out alive   you have to keep going
until you find something   otherwise none of the
dying means anything

self talk

the world is opulent and multitudinous and i am glad
to be in it exclamation mark i am standing here in my
burgundy dressing gown and big socks and i will
continue to do so except i will also get dressed and perhaps
leave the apartment   i will drink a hot cup of coffee
and enjoy the feeling of slightly increased energy it imbues
me with exclamation mark   i will listen to the recording of
somebody's voice accompanied by musical instruments
and i will let it have a strong impact
on my mood   i will look out the window and pretend
everybody else is listening to the same voice accompanied
by musical instruments   and life is becoming increasingly
generous   like an after-school special from 2003
            i will walk through the city and pet all of the cats   i will
do something momentous and ethically powerful   or at least
i will do a hundred small things   that add up to one slightly
bigger but still quite insignificant thing   i will wonder
      how many small things i have to do to add up
to something impactful   question mark   i will
lie awake at night counting them   i will avoid newspapers
and then   i will feel guilty for avoiding newspapers
      i will remind myself again   that the world is abundant
and we have everything
            we could ever need   exclamation
mark

something better

eat an orange in the sun lightly peel it apart
each part sticky & lined with pith I swear
eating citrus in late summer's like being alive
two warm bodies in a big white bed
I've been sleeping later lately soaking in
my skin as the sun sidles through the window

//

early autumn spent insulating my chest
an attempt to keep the warmth in my hands
still sticky with light turned into sugar
into something better
turn with the seasons and the dark
coffee in a blue cup emanating a tiny sun
turning the flowerheads bloom
like paint in oil as they're
visited by honeybees for the last time

//

a fullness in the throat
I bruise like a peach
and the language won't come what kind of
sustenance is this what kind of half life
are we living drink a cup of palm oil
let it slick my stomach empty as a vase
and call it soup or something better

me & you & you & you

i want to walk around with you
       and be looked at   i like
to be looked at
but if you look at me the wrong way   i will not like it

it's up to you to know the right way
       i want to walk around by myself and be invisible
but look at my reflection
in the windows of the shops i pass
           i want to see myself reflected in your pupils
      and a tiny image of you reflected
         in the pupils of my reflection
and so on and so on
      until there are hundreds of us
         growing infinitely smaller
doing nothing but looking

      and even after all of this
i still get shy when i undress
      i think if you stop looking at me like that i might die
      but then i get up and
am alive again
      but i will not let you look at me anymore
i will not even video-call you
and look at myself   in the little box in the corner
because i might see you reflected in my face

          i don't want to be bearable for you
     i want to be a disembodied voice

                filling the air and floating   omniscient and all-powerful
telling you how much i like your shirt

whenever i see someone on a bike
i think it's you
        even if you're in another city
                even if you are walking beside me

there are hundreds of you
        riding red bicycles around the streets of wellington
and i am looking at all of you
                you are moving towards me
and   away from me at the same time
you are moving very fast and giving way
to another you   you are turning into the sunlight
                you are not looking at me
        you are not even looking

2050

Carbon capture may indeed prove to be 'magical thinking', but the cruder technologies – we know these will work. Rather than sucking carbon out of the atmosphere, we could shoot pollution into the sky on purpose; perhaps the most plausible version involves sulfur dioxide. —David Wallace-Wells

I pay daily attentions to colour
                    7am waiting at the bus stop under
                             a sulphur-red sky
              burnt at the edges where it
                       sticks to the horizon
fading to a midday dull white sheen

        the ocean a room of
mirrors reflecting itself
        the edges of waves tinged pink
                    like we're on another planet
but we're exactly
        where we've always been

except there's a PE teacher
pushing us to go faster than we want to
                    jogging into an apocalyptic future
                             in polyester shorts

what if kids dare each other to stand
                             outside in the rain
knowing the trees burn faster now
        having watched a video at school
                    of red flames on a red sky
        shot in slow motion

what if   above our heads
we project squares of blue
with white blurs passing across

something missing at the core but
        the absence imperceptible
to the human eye

I could count the shapes as they pass
        I could
come to love them
        against a false sky
I'm afraid
        I could forget
there was ever another way

crocodile tears

                         sometimes I love him
so much I have to laugh at myself
                but what does it matter
the earth wobbles
                like a spinning top

astronauts on the moon
                                        could reach out
        thumb and forefinger
and give it another spin

if the moon was really cheese
        we would have
        cut it up and eaten it by now
I used to cry so much I worried
                        I'd make the ocean bigger
we do the most damage while awake

if we could all
        go to the moon   one by one
and look back
        we wouldn't live like this

                        public weeping
        is a political statement
                I could send up flares
but they'd be mistaken for fireworks
        and upset the neighbourhood pets
we have to find healthier ways

      to come to terms with devastation
but it can't involve
      asking ourselves to stop

      listen
if you were dead   and some kids
      stood in front of a mirror
with the lights off   and said
your name three times
      could you face them

pool party

if you will not share your planet   I will go
& make my own   & you are not allowed
on it   it will be sweet & idyllic
my planet will have a moat   & my friends and I
will go swimming every day & brush each other's hair
until it shines

                                        we will carry
our oxygen tanks around
all the time   & make something fashionable
of them   & how many moons shall we have
      how many ways shall we soften the world to
meet us   will our bodies always yearn
for the place we belong

on my planet   just as on Earth   newly hatched turtles
will head for the ocean   tiny flippers
going everywhere   trying to make contact
with a home they've never known

people like contained fires are just walking around
trying not to be put out
as the body enacts the trauma of the mind
      the planet's moat deepens & swells
the hair-brushing becomes difficult   as the rocks
we used to sit on   are swallowed up
& our glamour diluted
      before long   we start drawing up
plans for a new planet   without the design flaws
of the last

saying your names

after Richard Siken

the earth has names in every language / in
body language, an unravelling, the self offered,
open-faced and blushing, leaves flat and
extended, tender / since the beginning of human
thought / we've been drunk with naming,
with godly names, secret names / true names
with absolute power / animal names, not scientific
but the names wild beasts give the world, guttural
and warm, worn in the throat, irresistible /
inexpressible, but we're trying, gesturing
at the sky and the ground, like babies learning
to speak, imitate, repeat, we learn the sounds
other people respond to / the more we love
a thing the more names it has, like the sun,
my emotional support star, my long-distance
lover, the original hot girl, the inventor
of sunsets, wildfire / if you look directly at it
everything dissolves / each name gets closer
but refracts / like looking through a prism, light
glancing everywhere, refusing to be held

transplanting

for Dorothy Wordsworth

in her body   I walk to Rydal Lake   gather foxgloves
come home for tea & write the names of trees
        sycamores & firs & a grove of hazels
I mend her brother's clothes   help build the fire
        I practise diligence in the face of her life

look in the mirror & the vision fills with white noise
        the shape in the glass like
trying to count my fingers in a dream

in this year   I pause halfway up Mt Vic to catch my breath
        who was the last woman in my family who could name
each of these trees by sight?   trees unknown to Dorothy or me
        dirt under our fingernails   trying to rebuild our bodies
with the land & the land with our bodies

I take the pot with the plant that died during transplant
        empty it in the corner of the lot   & hope nobody looks out
to see me abandoning it there under its own dirt

it takes more than one human lifetime for a forest to grow

a glass bowl breaks on my kitchen floor & Dorothy bends down
        picks up the shards as thick as my thumb   wraps them
in sheets of paper & flourishes the bouquet
afterwards   our fingers bloom red with tiny incisions

taxonomic loss

I call a body a body / I call a name but the named thing has
vanished / grey whales / from the Atlantic / their name
meaningless to them / salt water rushes to fill the absence /

how easily language dissolves / a voice decanted / to know
and to name are different urges / to go about the day feeling
mammalian / to feel the sky on my back / see the atmosphere
as a tent / and let that be enough /

the scientific name for deer mice is *peromyscus* / which
comes from the Ancient Greek *pero* for boots / and *mys* for
mouse / translating roughly to *mouse with boots* / we're just
making this shit up /

I'm trying to stop looking at things from a distance / silent
rooms of articulated skeletons / wires in place of tendons /
sinew and cartilage gone / a golden plaque on the wall with
the *Linnaean* name inscribed / bones exposed and still / too
far away to discern /

umbilical

if you have held in your palm a fish   drowning in the open air
or swum deep underwater   felt the pressure build in your ears
and brain   you know how bodies can change

if a fantail flies a circular pattern   returning to the branch each time
to perform a serenade   it's trying to woo you
                                        you can politely decline

if a child starts swimming lessons as a baby   it's easier to begin
          the frog-like movements are still in recent memory   shrouded
in the darkness of the womb

if in the hospital   the nurse puts your blood in somebody else's
body   pink blooms in their cheeks again   their pulse
hammers on   thick tubes carry fluids directly to the vein
          as if from the placenta

back home   with the smell of bread in an oven   strands of gluten
sew together   flesh settling around minuscule pockets of air

if they find a mate   fantails build a nest and bind it with cobwebs
          spun to entrap   and salvaged for something just as delicate

still enclosed   the chick punctures the air bubble that lines the shell
          and takes its first breath   slick with amniotic fluid   the first
act is to break

good people

o soy milk carton   I just want to recycle you   I just want
you to go on & fulfil your life dreams
of being pulped
         & reused to make new cartons
& hold other consumable liquids   like orange juice   or almond milk
except we can't call almond milk
                  almond milk anymore
because it's too misleading   & causes innocent shoppers to
imagine almonds with tiny almond teats being milked by
almond farmers who get up at 4am everyday
         nobody wants to think about that while they do
their grocery shopping

         you can't be a good person even if you recycle
if only everyone didn't already have their own piles of used plastic
         maybe we could find someone to buy all of our piles of used plastic
                  synthetic clothes release
         particles into the ocean every time you wash them
& I have dreams of drowning in a sea of bubble wrap
while around me people lounge on cruise ships drinking
piña coladas & saying   But I Use Them For Bin Liners

I have dreams of me & all my friends buying
organic compostable faux-plastic wrap
while billionaires build single-use bouncy castles the size of islands
& we panic like housewives in the 80s doing bad jazzercise
choreography in front of the television while the house
burns down around us   pump those arms girls
         can you feel the burn yet

asparagus season

it arrives sometime in late September
in a shock of green and purple
          it makes me
weak at the knees in the supermarket aisle
               the row of spears
like an assembly of tiny men
          ready to go to war just for me

some days he brings it home in bouquets
and we cook risotto with plenty of white wine
          the hard beads of rice swirling
in the bottom of the pan

six weeks later
               the regiment is nowhere to be seen
               as the temperatures turn
          more callous each passing year

and every time   I know
I should have cherished it more while it was here
          bought armfuls and armfuls
for us to lay across the kitchen counter
               but it's a spring romance
               it burns bright and sweet
          and ends before it's really begun

I dream of growing it myself
               it's a vegetable to settle down with
when you're ready for something more long-term
          than the casual flings of supermarket crops

when cultivated
it becomes a slow-burning affair
                drawn out and teasing
with its spears pushing up from the bed each spring
        firm yet tender
the discipline of waiting three years before tasting

coming home to the same place every day
        and seeing the soil and sun and water
believing in the world three years from now
        as more than abstraction   not a mirage
but something liveable

marine snow

a coming-of-age film
                the crucial scene
            where I drift
through the water
            bubbles erupting
        from my nose   I want
to hold my breath   better
        than I can   stay in
                until my lips
turn blue

            when I was three   I hated swimming
                    I wouldn't take my feet off the floor
one day the instructor said
                        that a crab lived
on the bottom of the pool   it would
        pinch my toes
                I got out of the pool

does the last
            of anything know
            it's the last
we give it a human name
                    I'm not built
for this kind of grief
                I start to carry it
        around and put a little
                    into everything I do
        now

                    the pot of coffee
is in mourning   now
                    the laundry
      drips wet tears

                        did you know it
snows underwater   that's what
        we call it when bodies
fracture and sink   skin and scales
mixing
        with plankton and dust   I don't
want to eulogise anything
                              I want
        a name
            for the feeling

                              of never wanting
            to see something
        but being
                    glad

        it exists

farm wife

you come home and joke
that I'm your farm wife
         in my long brown skirt
and beige sweater
                  sleeves rolled up
to knead the bread
another loaf already
                  in the oven
I've spent the afternoon
         hanging sheets outside
to frolic in the wind
         and thinking about
which vegetables to plant
                  come spring
it's so romantic
         to wake up before dawn
and sit in the freezing mud
         milking cows
while a little farm cat
         jumps around
looking for farm mice
and to sit in the farmhouse
         after dinner
         darning socks
whatever that means
         and to catch up on
the latest farm gossip
such as
         which chickens have

stopped laying
who's planted tomatoes
      instead of waiting
           for one last frost
and to read about the latest
      farm crime
           until I go to bed
with you
      my farm husband
exhausted and content
      too tired to dream

carrying capacity

I don't ask for much   only everything
        in baby pink
a baby-pink dreamscape
        with baby-pink forests and lakes
                and a baby-pink house

a beach where I
        sit and look at the castles
built by kids earlier that day
                        before the tide
comes in like a good socialist
        and washes them away

I'm afraid Earth has reached her limits
        she wants to sleep through the night
I want to get home safe
        on this baby-pink airplane
the safety briefing said
        to wait until we've exited the plane
before inflating our life jackets
                but we pull the tabs too early
                        and the plane plummets

full of people who've suddenly doubled in size
                bouncing around
        like balloons in a broom cupboard
                the drinks cart rattling
        cheap champagne
spilling everywhere   emergency

exits all blocked up

in real life
        you can't afford to have a baby
but you still want to

in the movies
when someone misses their period
                        they panic
they pee on a plastic stick
        and then throw it away

party tricks

to show off to my friends I
steal thousands of Venus flytraps
from the only place they naturally grow
                in North Carolina

their delicate stems wrapped
around each other's heads   mouths closing
around mouths   as they're all
stacked together in a sack

I carry them away like
a burglar in an old cartoon
            the bulging cloth bag
over my shoulder

other times   I feed myself
to them
           fingering the leaves
until they snap shut over my skin

I emerge unscathed and smug
to looks of amazement from my friends
          while the trap waits
twelve hours to reopen

and after a few more false alarms
starvation creeps in
               spreading
across the leaves like a burn

leaving me
with nothing to show
and nothing to say
       except

my friends   if you like plants that bite
        wait until you hear about animals!
with their fully functioning digestive systems
and wide red mouths   full of teeth

washed up!

it gets tiring pushing the fire alarm every night
                                    but things keep catching on fire
or sometimes it's only a dream & we have to undo it all

                    send the firemen away!
                                    get everybody back to bed!

            wait for the ringing in our ears to fade
our clothes are heavy with the smell of smoke
                    even hanging on the line they look ashen & worn down
            like people on a cigarette break

we can get used to anything given enough time
                                            for example
it took 35 years for people to get used to hundreds of Garfield phones
            washing up on a French coast

they became part of the scenery
                    with dirt settled in the hollows of their eyes
                                    & nobody ever calling

imagine walking down the beach when one by one
                                            they all start to ring
        what a cacophony!   I pick up the receiver
        but there's nobody on the other end of the line

months later I wake in the middle of the night
            & think I hear it   that damn cat!
                    turns out it's just the fire alarm again

turns out   the walls are burning
        & I can't see them for the smoke

mating in suburbia

I'm woken by a bird screaming
on the peak of the roof

its throat punching in & out
in & out

that's just how it talks
this is how we talk

all hard touch & outpour
all ??????? & !!!!!!!!!

we dance in our underwear but then it gets cold
so we put our clothes back on

we dance in our skeletons but they start glowing in the dark
ribs sticking out like fishbones

we want to be more than just bodies
like a bird calling for a mate

when he hasn't finished
building his nest yet

he's cute but not practical
there's no time left for meaningless flings

we watch them without knowing their names
so each one is a brand new bird

on the fence or the washing line
not doing anything in particular

& at the kitchen window we are a small deluge of love
enamoured of his orange beak & stick legs

he doesn't know that today is a Wednesday
but I wonder if he can feel the quickening

the sludge of heat in the atmosphere
when summer should already be over

watching him our feelings get so big
we don't know how to talk about them

so instead they run adrift
shifting idly in the humid air

& we fall out of love with ourselves
& can't say why

worm food

let bones be bones
        let my body be undone
turn the soil
    rich and dark
undig each grave
        once the rain wets it
like a tongue
    pushed into the space
        left by a tooth
    let the roots
spread between my
    finger bones and
reach deeper
        follow the waters
    pull and pull
strengthen the spine
        and find new growth
    like fresh linen
        on the forest bed
first breaths
    first blooming
        wet mud of birth
beetles buried neck deep
    in flower heads
        their hunger indulgent
    the air humming
leaves thin and glistening
    watching over new and old
the ground opened

       and a body placed in
the ground opened
           and a seed sown

vegetable zodiac

I think I feel better when I'm not
counting the days   let's find
old ways of keeping track   the potatoes are up
and we're moving again
          romancing each other
with bouquets of kale   the broccoli has bolted and I'm
very in love   with its long-legged swaying
          yellow heads mocking our hunger   get
the zucchini seedlings in the ground and try
letting your mind germinate   I have faith in the
vegetable zodiac   and in basil sprouting pairs
of leaves on top of each other until there's more
than we'll ever eat   find a soft patch
of ground to rest the pumpkin heads on
when they get too heavy for the vine   as a late
April baby I get along well with the
winter squash   lying down is an important part
of our process   especially when the days
grow short and indeliberate   and the mornings
at the market are a haze of rain with children
in yellow gumboots getting lost   until
the greens break through in spring

one third the weight of a mouse

i have to confess
that though we've been in love for years
i am actually 78 grey warblers in
jeans and a coat

each bird one third the weight of a mouse,
altogether the weight of 26 mice
getting up in the morning

and going to work on time
(and i don't ask to be paid
an hourly wage for each of my 78)

haven't you noticed how silky my feathers are,
how sharp my pecks on your cheek?
how much i squirm and shift about
next to you in bed,
each bird taking its time to get comfortable
in the nooks of your
elbows and knees?

either way, i hope you can forgive me
i might seem flighty but i'm here to stay
and i pay my taxes like anybody else
i never meant to take up space in your world
only there isn't much left in mine

love poems when all the flowers are dead

this is the start of a new poetry school   it's called ~Dinosaur Romanticism~

we write lines like
    I miss you like a long-dead pterodactyl misses the air rushing through its wings
&
    you make my body tremble like a much younger Earth under a T-Rex's feet
&
I'd swallow the comet whole for you
but it can't make them come back
here's my ode to a diplodocus   here's my meditation on brachiosaurus hearts
    it would have gone down well in the Late Jurassic era but it's no good as elegy

here's a pile of old bones lashed together +
                    a library like a graveyard with shiny new headstones

this poem is like a bird's broken rib   so small you'd never notice it
but once there's enough of them you'll start to hear it
            the gaps in the song

you can dress up a skeleton as much as you want but it still looks dead
you can hide the scent
you can come crying when your books are full of corpses
    & all your love poems are about birds that your children will never see alive
only dioramas in museums
            cold bones with the feathers hot-glued on

undergrowth

at dusk the birds by the road
are loud as a fire   so much noise
from such small lungs
            we say
it seems impossible but what's worse is
we should be able to hear this anywhere
                        the branches
always ripe with nests
        in spring

birdsong so big
we could dance to it
        but the next day
we're overheating
        & everyone's too busy worrying
to notice our spot under the trees
        I'm imagining a giant ballroom with
        this leafy canopy for a roof
the floor a pool of cool green light

                nobody's been here for centuries
most of the birds are gone too
but an ant crawls
across the cracked marble
        & somewhere in the silence our buried
forms turning
                back into earth   are still
in love
& the flowers pick themselves
        up & carry on

stray cats

we get used to the sound   of water
running through a wall   so close-
quartered we're almost sharing
body heat with the neighbours   we can
see their voices arranging themselves
on the couch   and the doorways
shrink at night so the doors pop
when they finally give   and flecks of paint
snow onto the carpet

                                      people are
hard to live with   people are hard to
live without   wanting to paint
the walls blush pink   and put shelves up
        dig up the garden and plant asparagus
        disrupt the layers of stagnant air and
the ghosts still living here   she
never opened the windows   he
grew succulents and then
                        left them to die

I read a story about a woman
        who moved into a house
and found it came with nine cats
who lived underneath
                when I moved in
I didn't know I was adopting a plant graveyard
and the mould loitering in the kitchen

do any other animals move so often?
          it's like a hundred stray cats
turning up to a flat viewing   hoping
somebody might toss them a scrap
          the half-rotten and unwanted
                    coming out
with nothing   but the clothes we wear
and wet lungs   the house with walls
that never stopped dripping   the one
with astroturf for carpet

                              you and I could learn
to coexist with the mice   but even they
don't want to live here   once you find
a place that feels like home you bury yourself
there   once you find somebody
who feels like home you bury your face
in their neck   expel the scent
of damp from your lungs
          inhale and picture something
better for yourself   blu-tac it
to the bedroom ceiling   hoping not to leave
a permanent mark

public holiday

the afternoon surfaces as a series of frames   white walls
painted with the shadows of plants   the internal window
between the kitchen & the dining room   through which I
watch you washing dishes   the sun comes in from the left
in measured diagonal lines   the wholeness
of the moment floods in   comes abruptly to a head
the fridge gurgles to itself   drawing attention away
from the things people are not supposed to see   blood or
          lungs filling with grey air   in the distance
tomorrow's storms gather themselves   amassing the energy
to hurry through   the mint lonely in its terracotta pot
          coming back to life   the loneliness I project onto
the mint   from my human body   in the habit of
coexisting   in the dining room   looking through to you
in the kitchen   noticing time waver & then   stand still

the Eremocene

... the planet will continue to descend irreversibly into the Anthropocene Epoch, the biologically final age in which the planet exists almost exclusively by, for, and of ourselves. I prefer to call this option by another name, the Eremocene, the Age of Loneliness. —E.O. Wilson

tonight for the first time
you are the only person in the house
only your lungs taking in this particular air
only your porch light on and mothless

       if somebody speaks in a room and nobody is there to hear
       if somebody lives in a room and nobody speaks
       if anybody speaks in a body and there's no room to live
       if nobody speaks in a room and somebody lives

the slightest noise punctures the silence
you flinch like a bird in fright
without knowing
the shudder of wings

       if you speak in a room is it lived in
       if some bodies cannot speak in a room are you listening
       if any bodies live is there room for them
       if you live is anybody here to hear you

choose your own adventure / poem

I sit on the turntable & spin all day
      all day long   I spin
lift my face
in fluorescent lights
      circles of colour slide off my head &
down my cheeks   each day
the body writes itself

      out of the body / into the body

      it remembers all
the bodies it has been
      doll–like
I wind myself back
wouldn't you rather be

      in outer space / anywhere else

      crickets spread through the house
they cling
      to the bedsheets
& blink

      in the light / in response

they leave a space
      the shape of a

      human / note pinned to a white satin pillow

I want to feel
it in my body afterwards
        that I've done something
              feel it

        like a workout / like an illness

wake up to

        apathy / atrophy / entropy

stand up & feel faint

        at 16 / at 22 / at 60

thinking of what we've

        given up / held on to

                              nursing the
        hurt like a sliver of glass under
the skin   invisible yet
unrelenting &   slow
dancing in the kitchen
        like somebody's

        turning away

night pollinators

watching the moths skirt the lampposts   you want to be someone
else   they dance in long grey drapes like a woman in a movie
who sews her own dress from the curtains   but forgets to
shake the dust off   night work is lonely   but throughout the
hemisphere   there are orchids blooming in the dark   there are
people who can't sleep   looking through photographs
          of when they were six years old   gorging themselves
on plums all afternoon   plucking them   heavy and overripe
straight from the tree   a city is on fire
          for the third time in a month   and somebody somewhere
saw white flowers unfolding in silver light   and named them
for the moon   an hour before sunrise you fall asleep
          your shoulders sink into a bed of wet sand   and the moths
at the streetlights and the night-blooms alike   pick up
their skirts   and carry themselves home

in the future

I could be a hermit crab real estate agent   round up
all the empty shells & show prospective crabs through
     saying things like   this one has a little extra room
to grow into   &   isn't this pattern so modern chic

I want to have beautiful lines around my eyes   &
get all my years   keep them in a velvet-lined box
& release them one by one   remember the names of every
animal I've ever seen   then leave them alone

I want to watch the trees turn orange & gold in real time
     drink coffee when I'm 80   & find spiderwebs
laced with frost   & anchored to the window frames
     I want to take fresh flowers

to my grandmother's grave   while people go home
to their lovers   who wait for them with tea on &
good news   who cry out when they press their cold fingers
against the skin at their waist

I could give back all the hermit crabs' money
     with interest   see trees 10 times my age
     & never carve my name into anything   see my
body wear its days   with grace or without

wake up in our house in the middle of the night
alone in the bed   to find you standing outside
     staring up at the sky
          millions of stars still visible

haircut

I'm overconfident with cheap hairdressing scissors
in the kitchen   under the electric light
        with the blinds down
to save the moths some bewilderment
                        piles of hair dot the linoleum
        small brown mammals for whom
                                we are now responsible

outside   the rest of the world is making decisions
        and acting on them
and I'm here thinking about how romantic it is
                to own half a fridge

we dream we can keep out the weather
        by keeping the windows shut
                        and down the street
                        so does everybody else

        as the lens widens
                the centre pulls back
see the line of apartments each with kitchen lights on
        somebody sautés onions in a frying pan
and empties the skins   brown and round
                into the compost

someone rinses their rice
        the water-turned-to-milk swirling down the drain
somebody else finds a spider in the bathroom
and transfers it to the back step alive

their hands shake but they still
have to live with themselves

the scissors curve around your ear
   and bring themselves back together
with a metallic whisper
     tiny shards of clipped hair cling
  to the skin as if magnetised

we get through the evening   it doesn't save us
but it does not mean nothing
    the weight of the blinds pulls on the string
  the spiders dart into the dark

52 hertz whale

the sound fills the room like light fills a swimming pool
   my ears ache under the pressure
of the recording played back for millions of people
who can also follow the migration patterns
plotted across the map on the screen

we love an underdog especially when it's a whale
we see ourselves in them literally in them lounging
in their cathedral of a mouth just looking for love
   like all the 30-something emotionally unfulfilled women
in Hollywood rom-coms what if none of the other
fish in the sea are on your frequency the wide ocean populated
with millions of bodies and not a single one
understands you

I worry that we'll learn the other whales can hear it singing
and suddenly I'll stop caring why don't we
pay this much attention to other whales happily finding
each other and having really big whale sex before moving on
to the next as dictated by regular whale mating patterns

their song isn't made to fit in human ears its reverberations
are too big and it leaves me feeling hollow
like I'm eavesdropping on an ancient
conversation but every year we keep
tuning in shaking our heads
  collectively holding our breath
our big collective human breath

water levels

the lights are off   because the fan makes too much noise   so it's dark
except for a few blooms from cheap tea candles on the vanity
and the windowsill   I close my eyes and you rub shampoo into my hair
    like parents do when you're a kid   I cup my hands and raise them
filled with water   a tiny bath for a tinier person who is washing
the hair of their beloved   and carefully wiping the soap bubbles
from their forehead   I hold them with a calm determination so as
not to spill their bathwater   you sit back and the water sloshes up
the ceramic wall and spills over the edge   because I filled it up too much
    or because the giant person holding this moment has small hands
it's a new kind of intimacy to know whose fingers wrinkle into prunes first
    and to discuss the benefits of conditioner   I lie back and
put my head under and the sound of your voice is muffled   my heart
pulses an emphatic beat   on its underwater drum
    you tell me our fingers and toes wrinkle
so we can hold on better in the water   which is good to know for when
the sea levels rise   the bathwater is starting to go cold   and when
I take out the plug I imagine the giant parting their hands very slightly
    to let the water pour out the gap in between   and it recedes
like the tide while I sit very still   so that I don't upset the balance

love poem with aphids

every morning I am thankful that you are not
                                    hundreds of bees swarming
            in the form of a person
                    hovering outside by the back door
your body buzzing so loudly
                    I can't even ask you to stay
you lift your arm to wave goodbye
                    as I draw the curtains in the evening

imagine trying to hold hands on the bus
                                    like how two people are never
        really touching
because of the invisible force between their atoms
                    except we could never even almost touch
because you are a swarm of bees
                    I'd plant lavender and marigolds in the backyard
leave all the windows open and spend July sick in bed
            carry bottles of sugar-syrup in case you get tired

                                    every morning I am thankful
                                        that the extinction event
didn't hit overnight
                    and we can turn off the alarm and steal
five minutes unfurling
                    next to each other in the cold sunlight
pale yellow and too much
            we open the curtains and wait
                        for the blackbirds to arrive in the trees
        I spend hours

picking aphids individually off a houseplant
                                        its stems dressed unfashionably
in their bright green fur

                              the atoms that make up my fingers
almost brushing against
                                                the atoms of their
      tiny bodies
but never quite touching

extant

i wake in the night with phantom pains
in the limbs of lost species / first,
the avian twinge deep in the scapula,
spine curved forward, shoulders drawn up
and elbows folded in / turning away
from the ground / the subconscious responds
with recurring dreams of flight /

next, the sense of sinking into bathwater
as homecoming / the skin thins, the line
between within and without
barely present / remembering how light travels
through water, my body slows with it /
hair and fingers branching / memories
of certain muscles, long unused,
breach the surface / what am i
but a nervous system /

i remember a clearing,
a woman and a doe
stood frozen / soft hairs on the nape of the neck
picking up shifts in the air, head still and alert,
breathing quick / we both saw
and knew we were seen / i would not
be the first to move / i would
make myself slight, a shade /

morning comes, and pneumatic bones
fill in /gills smooth back into skin / bruises
purpling the legs with the iridescence
of beetles / i start slowly / each movement
an elegy / each breath
a thousand breaths not taken /

Notes

'walking with Dorothy': The lines in italic are taken from Dorothy Wordsworth's *Grasmere and Alfoxden Journals*, edited by Pamela Woof (Oxford University Press, 2002).

'location, location': NASA's climate modelling shows that Venus may have once had habitable temperatures and the surface conditions to support human life, before global warming led to its current conditions. climate.nasa.gov/news/2475/nasa-climate-modeling-suggests-venus-may-have-been-habitable/

'2050': The epigraph is from *The Uninhabitable Earth: A Story of the Future* by David Wallace-Wells (Allen Lane, 2019), p.107. In the book he discusses geoengineering as one possible solution to global warming. Though this idea has been largely dismissed, it is still pursued by some. Geoengineering technology would halt the warming of the planet by pumping chemicals into the sky that reflect sunlight away from Earth, but the air pollution levels would have a terrible impact on people's lifespans. Large amounts of sulphur dioxide would also make a lot more acid rain, and would change the colour of the sky.

'party tricks': In 2014, stealing Venus flytraps became a felony in North Carolina. The increased punishment came as a response to frequent incidents of mass poaching, which were damaging the natural population.

'washed up!': Novelty phones shaped like Garfield have been washing up on the shoreline of Brittany in Western France for over 30 years. They've been tracked to a lost shipping container from the 1980s.

'one third the weight of a mouse': The title comes from the Department of Conservation's description of the grey warbler/riroriro. doc.govt.nz/nature/native-animals/birds/birds-a-z/grey-warbler-riroriro/

'the Eremocene': This poem is inspired by E.O. Wilson's idea of the Eremocene, which he defines in *Half-Earth: Our Planet's Fight for Life* (Liveright, 2016) as the approaching age in which the only life left on Earth is human, and the animals used by humans to sustain ourselves – livestock and industrial crops.

'52 hertz whale': Since 1989, researchers have been tracking a whale whose song is unique in its frequency at 52 Hz. This might mean that other whales are unable to hear it. Its migration patterns are most similar to blue whales or fin whales, but otherwise we know almost nothing about it.